Stores and Retail Spaces 7

From The Institute of Store Planners and the Editors of *VM+SD* magazine

ST MEDIA GROUP INTERNATIONAL

CINCINNATI, OHIO

ISBN: 0-944094-51-1

Published by:
ST Books
ST Media Group International Inc.
407 Gilbert Avenue
Cincinnati, Ohio 45202
P: 513-421-2050 | F: 513-421-6110
E-mail: books@stmediagroup.com
www.stmediagroup.com/stbooks

Distributed to the U.S. book and art trade by:
Watson-Guptill Publications
770 Broadway
New York, NY 10003
www.watsonguptill.com

Distributed outside the U.S. to the book and art trade by:
Collins Design, *an Imprint of* HarperCollins*Publishers*
10 East 53rd Street
New York, NY 10022
www.harpercollins.com

Book design by Kim Pegram, Art Director, VM+SD
Book written by Jenny Reising, Freelance Writer
Book edited by Steve Kaufman, Editor, VM+SD;
Matt Hall, Managing Editor, VM+SD and
Alicia Hanson, Associate Editor, VM+SD

Printed in China
10 9 8 7 6 5 4 3 2 1

Stores and Retail Spaces 7

From The Institute of Store Planners and the Editors of *VM+SD* magazine

For 34 years, retailers, designers and architects from all

over the world have entered their finest projects into the

ISP/VM+SD International Store Design Competition.

Members of the Institute of Store Planners gathered

together to determine the best in retail excellence from

a variety of diverse submissions.

Here are those recognized winners from the

2004 ISP/VM+SD International Store Design Competition.

Contents

Fornarina

Mandalay Place, Las Vegas

SPECIALTY RETAILER,
SALES AREA 1501 TO 3000 SQ. FT.

*First Place (Tie) and
Store of the Year*

Throughout Europe, in China and in its one previous U.S. location in Los Angeles, Fornarina had gone for an elegant, understated format in which to present its fashion shoes and apparel.

Architect Giorgio Borruso changed all that for the store's new show-place in Las Vegas, which was named Store of the Year in the 2004 ISP/VM+SD International Store Design Competition.

"Las Vegas is a place that invites risk," Borruso says. "It challenges you to do something different."

Borruso's design for Fornarina was certainly different, a departure from any of the retailer's other stores. He created a tactile experience full of organic forms and shapes, hypnotizing colors, surrealism, sensuality and a sense of movement. But the overall sensation is restful and soothing.

"Our objective was to create an oasis inside the chaotic bustle of the Mandalay Bay Resort & Casino," says Borruso, "a place of rest for the retina and the mind, a place to retire and feel comfortable."

The unusual blends with the expected. So the rich complex shapes offer clear and concise merchandise presentations, such as the perfectly circular shoe platforms inside organic silicon oval elements; or the smooth, tactile surfaces in cool pearlescent colors. The undulating floor, created from custom-made textured vinyl, produces what Borruso regards as an "oneiric," dreamy experience. And the unusual lighting elements hanging from the ceiling – what Borruso calls "tentacles" – support grids of directional lights and LED color effects that turn the store a moody red once a day.

Even the signature Fornarina fuchsia, dominant in its other stores, becomes an accent color in Borruso's design.

CLIENT
Fornari USA, Los Angeles – Sergio Azzolari, ceo; Edward Kangeter, vp; Adrienne Weller, director of communications, visual merchandising

DESIGN AND ARCHITECTURE
Giorgio Borruso, Marina del Rey, Calif.

ARCHITECT-OF-RECORD
Gensler, San Francisco

GENERAL CONTRACTOR
Fineline Group, San Francisco

LIGHTING
North Shore Consulting, San Francisco

FLOORING
Lonseal, Carson, Calif.

FURNITURE AND FIXTURES
T. Alongi, Montreal

FIBERGLASS/RESIN
BamBam Designs, City of Industry, Calif.

TENTACLES/FABRIC DRESSING ROOM
Eventscape, Toronto

DOOR HANDLES
PRL Glass Systems, City of Industry, Calif.

SIGNAGE AND GRAPHICS
Y.E.S., Las Vegas

PHOTOGRAPHY
Benny Chan/Fotoworks, Los Angeles

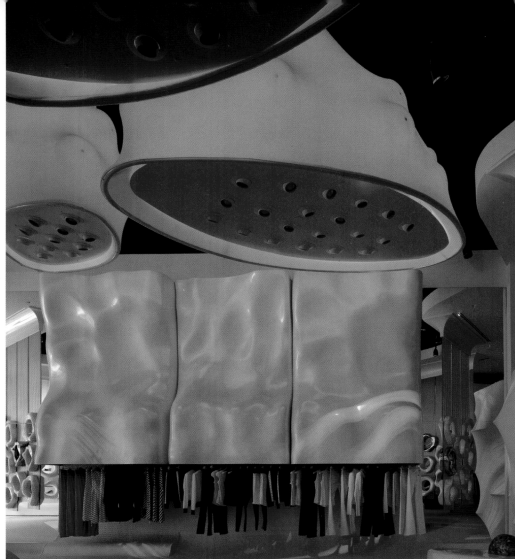

Lotte
Department
Store

Daegu, South Korea

NEW OR COMPLETELY RENOVATED
FULL-LINE DEPARTMENT STORE

First Place

Distinctly international in flavor, the new Lotte Department Store in Daegu, South Korea, beckons its young, affluent clientele from the outside in. The use of metal panels and colored lighting on the semi-circular, glass-encased exterior tower isn't just eye candy: Each color delineates a service and floor.

Inside the eight-story mall, natural and high-tech materials, bright and subdued colors blend seamlessly to create a contemporary, attractive environment. Light, open and airy describes the children's floor, which features key aisle focals, curved shapes, bright colors and interesting ceiling treatments. In the young women's department, fashion takes center stage – literally. Faux brick and metal "stages" allow mannequins to model clothing on mini-runways. And a dramatic wall merchandising system – complete with bold lighting, innovative fixturing and compelling graphics – adds to the theatrical look. Even the produce department gets the full floor-to-ceiling design treatment with oversized graphics overhead.

CLIENT
Lotte Department Store, Sang-In, South Korea – Kyuk-Ho Shin, chairman; In-Won Lee, president; Hee-Tae Kang, general manager, merchandising strategy; Kil-Young Park, chief designer; Hyeong-Se Soe, senior project designer

DESIGN AND ARCHITECTURE
FRCH Design Worldwide, Cincinnati – Jim Lazzari, principal-in-charge/partner; Andrew McQuilkin, vp, design; Jeanine Storn, design director; Young Rok Park, senior designer; Heesun Kim, designer; Sonya Davis, resource design; Denette Callahan, project manager; Tim Goyette, professional

GENERAL CONTRACTOR
Lotte Construction Team, Sang-In, South Korea

PHOTOGRAPHY
Kwang-Sik Kim, Seoul, South Korea

Almacenes Paris

La Florida, Santiago, Chile

NEW OR COMPLETELY RENOVATED
FULL-LINE DEPARTMENT STORE

Award of Merit

Designers pulled out all the stops for the new three-level, 150,000-square-foot Almacenes Paris store in Santiago, Chile. Square columns and curved ceiling panels dominate the cosmetics department and serve as architectural signatures; blue back-painted glass panels reinforce the brand at the escalator; and colorful, backlit lifestyle graphics are visual beacons in every department.

CLIENT
Almacenes Paris, Santiago, Chile – Alvaro Valdes, general manager; Maria Pia Rosso, project manager
DESIGN
RYA Design Consultancy, Dallas – Tom Herndon, partner and ceo; Jeff Henderson, senior associate/project director; Robert Coker, senior project designer
PHOTOGRAPHY
Alfredo Gildemeister, Santiago, Chile

Bloomingdale's

SoHo, New York

NEW OR COMPLETELY RENOVATED
SPECIALTY DEPARTMENT STORE

First Place

To affirm its commitment to downtown Manhattan, Bloomingdale's selected the building formerly occupied by Canal Jeans as its satellite flagship in New York. The 90,000-square-foot mid-19th Century brick building on lower Broadway needed some work, but it had solid architectural bones that designers at the now-defunct Tucci, Segrete + Rosen used to full advantage when creating the space.

Building on the idea of a "visual storyline," designers at Bloomingdale's and TS+R blended exposed brick walls, oak flooring and tin ceilings with contemporary materials and functional displays to give the six-story space interest on every level. Designers maximized light by refurbishing existing skylights and light wells, uncovering previously concealed windows, installing a new double-wide entrance on Crosby Street and creating a three-story atrium at the Broadway entrance. Pink cosmetics bars and checkerboard flooring make an impression at the main-floor cosmetics area, while a pale blue palette and black and white photographs mark the third-floor contemporary collection. In the lower-level men's department, graffiti-style hand-painted murals give the space a retro-80s feel.

CLIENT
Bloomingdale's/Federated Department Stores, Cincinnati – Jack Hruska, senior vp, store design and visual merchandising; Shan DiNapoli, vp, store planning and design; Diane Koester Sibert, project director; Rudy Javosky, senior vp, design and construction; Bernie Reiss, divisional vp, design and construction; Bob Kapellas, operating vp, construction; Bill Stidum, project manager; Mike Pardee, senior project manager; Glen Withrow, Lance Woodard and John Schlageter, construction managers; Jeff O'Hearn and Elizabeth Grossman, project coordinators, purchasing

DESIGN AND ARCHITECTURE
Tucci, Segrete + Rosen, New York – Evangelo Dascal, president and project director; Edward Calabrese, executive vp, creative director; Lisa Contreras, senior vp, creative resources and development; Marco Oppici, senior project designer; Doug Griffin, project manager

ARCHITECTURAL/ENGINEERING
Highland Associates, New York

GENERAL CONTRACTOR
SPACE – Federated Department Stores, Cincinnati

LIGHTING
Horton Lee Brogden, New York

AUDIO/VISUAL
Crow's Nest Entertainment, New York

CEILINGS
US Gypsum, New York

FIXTURES
Monarch Industries, Warren, R.I.; Suss Woodcraft, Montreal; Builders Furniture, Winnepeg, Man.

FLOORING
Innovative Marble & Tile, New York

FURNITURE
Cassina, New York; Barret Hill, New York; Dakota Jackson, New York; Steelcase, New York

MANNEQUINS
Adel Rootstein Mannequins, New York; Patina-V, City of Industry, Calif.

PHOTOGRAPHY
Mancini•Duffy, New York

Barneys New York Chelsea Passage

New York

NEW SHOP-IN-SHOP WITHIN AN
EXISTING FULL-LINE OR SPECIALTY
DEPARTMENT STORE

First Place

*This project also won a
Special Award for innovative
merchandising*

When converting 15,000 square feet of Barneys' back-of-house space into destination retail at its Madison Avenue store, designers used attractive lighting, curved fixturing and an inventive materials palette to create a well-appointed, loft-like space. The home furnishings department, called Chelsea Passage, houses everything from tableware, home accessories, gifts and stationery to bridal, linens and kids' clothing.

To unify this vast product range, designers got creative – and had a little fun. A series of 32-foot-long, undulating, internally illuminated shelves display art glass; formal place settings are mounted on nickel-silver "potato chips" set into a curved wall; and a sculptural steel fixture system houses clothing in the kids' department. And the breathless list of materials runs the gamut from teak, oak, rosewood and sycamore veneers to marble, Venetian plaster, concrete, aluminum honeycomb, cork and industrial felt. To add to the high-end, art-infused atmosphere, Barneys worked with designers to create a series of installations, including a 26-foot-wide entry gate with laser-cut aluminum sculptural panels and column-mounted wire stork sculptures in kids.

CLIENT
Barneys New York, New York – David New, evp, creative services; Tracy Edwards, vp, Chelsea Passage

DESIGN AND ARCHITECTURE
TPG Architecture LLP, New York – Michael Hayes and Vincent Iacobellis, principals-in-charge; Alec Zaballero, associate principal, design director; Milosh Seckulich, RA, senior associate, project manager; Marina Benfield and David Gomez, designers, Eric Mailaender and Vera Nediko, project architects

GENERAL CONTRACTOR
OD&P, New York

LIGHTING
Johnson Schwinghammer Lighting, New York

AUDIO/VISUAL
Ambrosino dePinto & Schmieder, New York;
ECI Communications Corp., S. Plainfield, N.J.

CEILINGS
Barrisol, New York

FIXTURES
Otema, Markham, Ont.

FLOORING
Stone Source, New York; Hawa Bamboo Flooring Corp., Sayerville, N.J.

PHOTOGRAPHY
Mark LaRosa, Brooklyn, N.Y.

Harrods, Designer Studio

Harrods, Knightsbridge, London

NEW SHOP-IN-SHOP WITHIN AN EXISTING FULL-LINE OR SPECIALTY DEPARTMENT STORE

Award of Merit

This project also won a Special Award for innovative store planning

At the redesigned 10,000-square-foot Designer Studio at Harrods' landmark Knightsbridge store, fashionistas now enter through pink glass tunnels and meander through smoked-glass merchandising fixtures that connect such high-end collections as Marc Jacobs, Cacharel and Sonia Rykiel. Existing windows dressed in metal-bead and chain curtains allow natural light in while infusing a distinct '70s style to the space.

CLIENT
Harrods, London – Mohamed Al Fayed, owner; Rik Dattani, store planning controller; Robert Flemming, retail development manager; John Akroyd , Averyl Oates

DESIGN
TPG Architecture LLP, New York – Louis Trudel, associate principal, project director; Inga Kruliene, associate principal, design director; Neal Kido, project architect; Marek Mastaj, senior associate, project manager, London; Cesar Cordero, associate, project manager, New York

GENERAL CONTRACTOR
Davies, London

OUTSIDE DESIGN CONSULTANTS
Gary Campbell Lighting Design, London (lighting); Anthony Jay Partnership, London (engineer); Logical Things Inc., New York (art direction/graphics/illustration)

VIDEO
Wow Factor, London

FIXTURES
Dula, Chertsey, U.K.

PHOTOGRAPHY
Harrods, London

The Paul Frank Store

**South Coast Plaza,
Costa Mesa, Calif.**

SPECIALTY STORE,
SALES AREA UNDER 1500 SQ. FT.

First Place

When Giorgio Borruso was commissioned to design a boutique store for retailer Paul Frank, his challenge was twofold: make the 1500-square-foot space open and flexible, and dream up a design that would reflect the unique merchandise: hip, modern and quirky but not slick. A floor-to-ceiling glass façade with a vertical graphic that reads "Paul Frank is your friend" welcomes visitors into the well-lighted store.

Inside, the retailer's trademark colors, orange, white, blue and black, dominate the space. To the right, behind the cashwrap, is a wall constructed of Douglas fir (one of Frank's mandates) that curves slightly at the bottom like a half-pipe. It features a flexible peg-like system that Borruso calls "a work in progress," where the owner can leave notes for customers or hang a bicycle. The cashwrap itself appears to spring from the wall in varying heights and curves, continuing the wave-like feel. To the left, colorful, modular freestanding and wall-mounted fixtures lend color, changeability and an element of surprise. Drawers pull out to create visual interest, while large, rolling fixture elements can be easily rearranged and colors can be combined in unique ways. And Frank's fun signature character, Julius, appears throughout the space, as an icon on the exterior signage and on a blue wall at the rear of the store.

CLIENT
Paul Frank Industries, Costa Mesa, Calif.
DESIGN
Giorgio Borruso, Marina Del Rey, Calif. – Giorgio Borruso, principal, designer
ARCHITECT
PBWS Architects, Pasadena, Calif.
GENERAL CONTRACTOR
Sneden + Bowers, Santa Ana, Calif.
FURNITURE AND FIXTURES
Studio Concepts, Long Beach, Calif.
FLOORING
Abet Laminati, Orange County, Calif.
SIGNAGE
Carey Sign Graphics, Anaheim, Calif.
PHOTOGRAPHY
Benny Chan/Fotoworks, Los Angeles

Bose @ Time Warner Building

The Shops at Columbus Circle, New York

SPECIALTY STORE,
SALES AREA UNDER 1500 SQ. FT.

Award of Merit

This project also won a Special Award for fixturing

The 1000-square-foot retail prototype for Bose features compelling graphics, a flexible merchandising system and curved walls and fixtures. Leather tile walls add warmth and texture to the space, and offer a rich backdrop to the high-style product. Automated sliding doors allow for sound demos in the rear theater, while baffles hidden in the ceiling absorb the sound.

CLIENT
Bose Corp., Framingham, Mass. – David Moody, project manager, store planning; Lori Hallahan, project manager, new business development; Joe Simanski, project manager, construction; Melissa Christou-Parker, marketing, retail group

DESIGN
Ædifica Inc., Montreal – Michel Dubuc, architect, partner-in-charge; Stéphane Bernier, senior designer; Nicolas Côté, senior designer; Marie-Josée Lapierre, project coordinator

AUDIO/VIDEO
Bose Corp., Framingham, Mass.

FLOORING/CEILING
Armstrong World Industries, Lancaster, Pa.

FIXTURES
Trial Design, Salaberry-de-Valleyfield, Que.

FABRICS
Knoll Textiles, East Greenville, Pa.

LIGHTING
Lightolier, Fall River, Mass.; LSI Lighting Solutions Plus, Cincinnati; Hera Lighting, Norcross, Ga.

SIGNAGE
Image National, Boise, Idaho

GRAPHICS
Contact Image, Montreal

LAMINATES
Nevamar, Odenton, Md.

WALLCOVERINGS
Benjamin Moore Paint Co., Montvale, N.J.; Black Stock Leather, Bethesda, Ont.; Stonyx Studio, Montreal

PHOTOGRAPHY
Courtesy of Ædifica Inc., Montreal

INNOVATION

AWARD-WINNING
SOLUTIONS INSPIRED
BY IMAGINATION.

O/3 Baby Collection

Harbour City; Tsim Sha Tsui; Kowloon; Hong Kong

SPECIALTY STORE,
SALES AREA UNDER 1500 SQ. FT.

Award of Merit

An all-glass façade and bright lighting draw customers into the new O/3 Baby Collection store, while striking blue signage and a liberal use of O/3's signature light blue reinforce the brand. The 700-square-foot store also features a curvilinear design and numerous pedestals, shelves and wall niches that put individual products prominently on display.

CLIENT
Danny Yuen, Hong Kong

DESIGN
IDesign (Intl.) Ltd., Hong Kong – Kelvin Law Kin-wai, creative director; Tony Yim, design assistant; Winnie Ho, design assistant

GENERAL CONTRACTOR
Ho Yin Decoration Engineering Co., Hong Kong

LIGHTING
Four Seas Engineering (HK) Ltd., Hong Kong

MANUFACTURER
OnLead, Guangzhou, China

LOGO
Fiat Advertising Production Ltd., Hong Kong

PHOTOGRAPHY
Freeman Wong, Hong Kong

Milli

Toronto

SPECIALTY STORE,
SALES AREA 1501 TO 3000 SQ. FT.

First Place (tie)

*This project also won a Special
Award for innovative finishes*

Charged with designing a fitting backdrop for Toronto retailer Milli's high-end clothing, II BY IV Design Associates went for full-on drama with a black and white palette. First, however, they had to contend with the downtown store's irregularly shaped space, high ceilings and peculiar location – in a corner laneway that is partially concealed by a park. By demolishing the doorway and canopy, designers opened up the façade to maximize the storefront, and incorporated flanking window displays to entice passersby.

Inside, white walls and limestone flooring contrast and complement the black details. A full-height front partition accepts merchandising fixtures below a huge acrylic rod wall sculpture that is animated by a programmable color LED light system. Two merchandising armoires line the side windows, which were sandblasted and blackened to sleek effect, while tall frames of deeply textured MDF in a glossy black finish reference the entry arch and surround matte wall panels that accommodate black glass shelves, hang rods or face-outs. Flexible workhorse fixtures throughout the space are designed for modularity: floor units can be moved easily for seasonal changes and special events; low black platforms are multi-purpose; and black lacquered boxes can be used to display a variety of merchandise.

CLIENT
Milli Gould, Toronto

DESIGN
II BY IV Design Associates Inc., Toronto – Dan Menchions; Keith Rushbrook

ARCHITECT
Giancarlo Garofalo Architect, Toronto

GENERAL CONTRACTOR
Structure Corp., Toronto

MECHANICAL/ELECTRICAL ENGINEER
MCW Consultants Inc., Toronto

FLOORING
Elte Carpets, Toronto; Ciot Marble & Granite, Concord, Ont.

MILLWORK/METALWORK
Deerwood Design Ltd., Brampton, Ont.

FABRIC
Kravet Canada, Mississauga, Ont.; Valley Forge Fabrics Inc., Pompano Beach, Fla.

LIGHTING
Interlight, Hamilton, Ont.; Eurolite, Toronto

FIXTURING
Marlite Canada, Woodbridge, Ont.

WINDOW GRAPHICS
LMS Canada, Toronto

FURNITURE
Louis Interiors Inc., Toronto

ACRYLIC SCULPTURE
Marc Littlejohn Inc., Toronto

METAL GRATE
Bolar/Ten Plus Architectural Products, Mississauga, Ont.

PLASTIC LAMINATE
Arborite, Toronto

WALLCOVERINGS
Metro Wallcoverings and Fabric, Toronto; Benjamin Moore, Toronto; Rodgers Wallcoverings Ltd., Toronto; Olympia Tile, Toronto

PHOTOGRAPHY
David Whittaker, Toronto

Reds Team Shop

**Great American Ball Park,
Cincinnati**

SPECIALTY STORE,
SALES AREA 3001 TO 5000 SQ. FT.

First Place

Tasked with capturing the rich 135-year history of the Cincinnati Reds baseball team in an open, fan-friendly environment, designers ensured that every fixture, graphic, lighting element and prop reinforces the notion of the Reds and baseball. Taking advantage of the 50-foot-tall glass façade, designers commissioned the creation of five oversized baseballs – representing the five Reds World Series victories – that are suspended from the ceiling on a circular chandelier with spotlighting for added drama when viewed from inside or out. The primarily white two-story space is peppered with red details that reinforce the team's colors. A high-gloss white porcelain floor with waterjet-cut red quartz baseball stitching leads fans through the space.

All fixturing, including the wishbone-shaped "C" cashwrap, features powdercoated steel, red granite countertops, red and white plastic laminate, textured glass panels and powdercoated screening that evokes the chain-link fence in the team's new Great American Ball Park. Red carpet and railing on the stairs bring visitors to the mezzanine, where signed memorabilia are displayed in locked, custom-designed, metal and glass cases. And 34-foot-tall, floor-to-ceiling Louisville Slugger baseball bats visually, and literally, connect the two floors.

CLIENT
Cincinnati Reds, Cincinnati

DESIGN
Retail Design Collaborative, Cincinnati –
John Heatherman
Jack Rouse Associates, Cincinnati – Amy Merrell; Brian Donahue

ARCHITECT
Architectural Group Intl., Covington, Ky.

GENERAL CONTRACTOR
Megan Construction Co. Inc., Forest Park, Ohio

LIGHTING
Abernathy Lighting Design Inc., N. Providence, R.I.

GRAPHICS
Geograph Industries Inc., Harrison, Ohio

AUDIO
RCA, Indianapolis

FIXTURES
Custom Millcraft Corp., Cincinnati; Marlite, Dover, Ohio

FLOORING
International Marble and Tile Inc., Hauppauge, N.Y.;
Mannington Commercial Carpets, Calhoun, Ga.

MANNEQUINS/FORMS/PROPS
Allen Meyer Ltd., Lake Zurich, Ill.

LARGE THEMED PROPS
The Nassal Co., Orlando

PHOTOGRAPHY
Matthew Lausé Photography, Cincinnati

Mickey's Star Traders

Magic Kingdom Theme Park, Lake Buena Vista, Fla.

SPECIALTY STORE,
SALES AREA 3001 TO 5000 SQ. FT.

Award of Merit

Mickey's Star Traders is a futuristic "Mickeyopolis." Oversized murals depict land, air, airships and trains. The sweeping ceiling comes to life with animated lighting, ending at a central "atomic energy" icon that beams light onto the floor and fixtures. And streamlined shapes, bold colors and careful placement of floor fixtures and wall bays extend the fantastic theme.

CLIENT
Walt Disney Parks & Resorts, Lake Buena Vista, Fla.
DESIGN/ARCHITECTURE
Walt Disney Imagineering/Global Retail Store Development, Lake Buena Vista, Fla. – Anthony J. Mancini, senior vp; Tom Sheldon, production (Orlando)
GENERAL CONTRACTOR
Vanson Enterprises Inc. Constructors, Winter Park, Fla.
LIGHTING DESIGN
Lighting Management, New City, N.Y.
FIXTURES
Themes & Concepts, Orlando; M.G. Concepts, Central Islip, N.Y.; Westco, New York
PHOTOGRAPHY
Lee McKee, Orlando

Big Shark Bicycle Company

St. Louis

SPECIALTY STORE,
SALES AREA 3001 TO 5000 SQ. FT.

Award of Merit

A new store design communicates the retailer's identity – a specialty bike shop that's passionate about the sport. A large expanse of glass invites customers into the store, which features graphic panels of store-sponsored cyclists, lighting that glows in a rich blue hue against wood framing and a custom fitting area for preferred customers.

CLIENT
Big Shark Bicycle Company, St. Louis – Mike Weiss, owner

DESIGN/ARCHITECTURE
Kiku Obata & Company, St. Louis – Kiku Obata, Kevin Flynn, AIA, Dennis Hyland, AIA and Troy Guzman, design team

GENERAL CONTRACTOR
Icon Contracting, St. Louis

OUTSIDE DESIGN CONSULTANTS
KPFF Consulting Engineers, St. Louis (structural engineers); William Tao & Associates, St. Louis (mechanical, electrical and civil engineers, plumbing, fire protection)

LIGHTING
Alkco, Franklin Park, Ill.; Metalux/Halo/Corelite, Houston; Surelite, Atlanta; Bruck Lighting, Costa Mesa, Calif.; Rambusch, New York; RSA Lighting, Chatsworth, Calif.

FIXTURES
Comatec, Weston, Ont.

CARPET
Pacificrest Mills, Irvine, Calif.

SECURITY SYSTEM
Vision Able, St. Louis; ABF/American Burglary & Fire, St. Louis

SIGNAGE AND GRAPHICS
Engraphix, St. Louis

PHOTOGRAPHY
Jon Miller, Chicago; Todd Owyoung, St. Louis

WOMEN'S

Lane Bryant

**Easton Town Center,
Columbus, Ohio**

SPECIALTY STORE,
SALES AREA 5001 TO 10,000 SQ. FT.

First Place

The focus is on fashion – and the plus-sized female shopper – at the new Lane Bryant store in Easton Town Center (Columbus, Ohio). The large, open space is light and airy, with a neutral color palette that doesn't compete with the high-style, colorful clothing. A "runway" traverses the middle of the store, reinforcing the fashion-forward feel and leading to the cashwrap, where a textured wall is emblazoned with the retailer's new signature Navajo Red. Throughout the store, plus-sized mannequins and black-and-white images of plus-sized models in the retailer's clothes give customers a realistic portrayal of how the merchandise will fit. Curved, fabric-covered light fixtures keep things bright and airy, while a drop ceiling above the intimates area offers comfort and privacy. Additionally, outfits and wardrobe concepts were grouped together by lifestyle, and store brands such as Cacique, Lane Bryant's intimate apparel line, are given their own space to make the store easy to navigate.

CLIENT
Lane Bryant, Reynoldsburg, Ohio – Tom Carr, store design director, Charming Shoppes; Kolby Veenstra, senior brand presentation manager, Lane Bryant; Jon Nubbemeyer, director of construction, Charming Shoppes; Mary Dawson, creative director, Lane Bryant

DESIGN
Chute Gerdeman, Columbus, Ohio – Mindi Trank, program director; Tony Oliver, creative director, environments; Steve Pottschmidt, design development director; Carmen Costinescu, materials specialist; Eric Daniel, creative director, graphics

ARCHITECT
CG Architecture, Columbus, Ohio

GENERAL CONTRACTOR
Construction One, Columbus, Ohio

CEILING
Interior Furnishing Merchandisers, Chagrin Falls, Ohio

FABRICS
Maharam, New York; Bernhardt Textiles, Lenoir, N.C.

FIXTURES
TC Millwork, Bensalem, Pa.; Garvey, Red Bank, N.J.

FLOORING
Crossville Porcelain Stone, Crossville, N.Y.

FURNITURE
Texstyle, River Vale, N.J.

LIGHTING
Amerlux, Fairfield, N.J.

MANNEQUINS/FORMS
Greneker, Los Angeles

DECORATIVE WALL PANELS
Modular Art, Mountlake Terrace, Wash.

WALLCOVERINGS
Benjamin Moore Paint Co., Montvale, N.J.; Sherwin-Williams, Garfield Heights, Ohio; MDC Wallcoverings, Elk Grove Village, Ill.

WOOD VENEERS
VenTec, Chicago

STOREFRONT CANOPY
Hanover Signs, Columbus, Ohio; Corporate Glass, Erie, Pa.

PHOTOGRAPHY
Eclipse Studios Inc., Dublin, Ohio

Coach

Marunouchi District, Tokyo

SPECIALTY STORE,
SALES AREA 5001 TO 10,000 SQ. FT.

Award of Merit

Feminine materials and an architecturally driven design mark the new Coach flagship in Tokyo. The exterior wall is replaced by glass, exposing a second layer of massive structural columns and floor slabs, and a third layer of vertical wood slats through which customers enter and exit. A materials palette of bleached walnut, limestone, white lacquer and glass keeps things light.

CLIENT
Coach, New York – Reed Krakoff, president/executive creative director; Michael Fisher, senior vp, global visual merchandising and store design; Michael Fernbacher, divisional vp, store design worldwide; Peter White. senior manager, international store design; Joy Bruder, director of visual merchandising international and wholesale; Julie McGinnis, director of design services; John Gunter, director of visual merchandising, Japan; Chris Amplo, director of store operations, Japan Kyoko Hasagawa, manager, visual merchandising international; Tsugio Kurosawa, project manager, Japan

GENERAL CONTRACTOR
Shimizu Corp., Tokyo

OUTSIDE DESIGN CONSULTANTS
Sato Facilities Consultants, Inc., Tokyo (project management); Worktecht, Tokyo (lighting)

FIXTURES
Soars Space Produce, Tokyo

PHOTOGRAPHY
Nacasa & Partners, Inc., Tokyo

Bailey Banks & Biddle

Houston

SPECIALTY STORE,
SALES AREA 5001 TO 10,000 SQ. FT.

Award of Merit

Bailey Banks & Biddle wanted a fitting flagship to convey its new motto
– "Where treasures live" – to its target consumer (35- to 45-year-old
women). A curved glass storefront and filigree grilled entryway lend a
residential feel, which continues with a comfortable seating area, neutral palette of cherry wood, fawn suede and brushed nickel and elegant
low-profile display cases.

CLIENT
Zale Corp., Irving, Texas – Mary Forté, president and ceo;
Sue Gove, evp/coo; Charles Fieramosca, president, Bailey
Banks & Biddle; Stephen Massanelli, svp/real estate;
Spencer Stovall, vp/property development; Parke Well-
man, director of store planning; Brenda Houston, director,
visual merchandising; Kurt Johnson, visual project man-
ager, Bailey Banks & Biddle

DESIGN
RYA Design Consultancy, Dallas – Tom Herndon, ceo/part-
ner; Mike Wilkins, creative director/partner; Chris Chavez,
project manager

FIXTURES
Faubion Associates Inc., Dallas

FURNITURE/UPHOLSTERY
Louis Interiors, Toronto; Momentum Textiles, Irvine, Calif.;
David Sutherland, Dallas; ID Collection, Dallas; Troscan,
Chicago; Pollack, New York

CARPET
Atlas Carpet Mills, City of Commerce, Calif.; Galerie
Diume, Paris

GLASS
Vision Products, Houston

LAMINATES
Wilsonart, Temple, Texas, Nevamar, Odenton, Md.

LIGHTING
Dongia, Dallas; Chista, New York

ENTRY GRILLWORK
Dallas Metal Fabricator, Dallas

MIRROR
Malloy Mirror & Art Glass Works, Dallas

PAINTS
ICI Paints, Berkshire, U.K.

STONE
Innovative Marble & Tile, Hauppauge, N.Y.

WOOD FLOORING
Buell Flooring Group, Dallas

WALLCOVERINGS
Studio E Inc., New York; Innovations in Wallcover-
ings, New York; Knoll Inc., East Greenville, Pa.; David
Sutherland, Dallas; Donghia, Dallas; Maharam, New
York; Elizabeth Dow Ltd., New York; Art People, New
York; Walter Lee Culp, Dallas; Southwest Progressive
Enterprises, Dallas

WOOD
Wood Gallery, Dallas; Architectural Systems, New York

PHOTOGRAPHY
Paul Bielenberg Associates, Los Angeles

REI

Portland, Ore.

SPECIALTY STORE, SALES AREA
10,001 TO 50,000 SQ. FT.

First Place

*This project also won a
Special Award for environmental
friendliness*

When relocating its Portland, Ore., store from the suburbs to a renovated industrial district downtown – surrounded by restaurants, art galleries and furniture stores – retailer REI hoped to bring its rugged, natural, eco-friendly sensibility to a decidedly urban audience. And while easy access for pedestrians, bicyclists and public transit riders was important, REI also wanted an interior design that would earn the retailer LEED certification for eco-friendliness.

Designers at Mithun achieved the retailer's trademark look with the use of unfinished surfaces – such as raw steel railings on the stair and unpainted concrete walls – and maximized natural light in the high two-story space through two all-glass walls and skylights. Sustainability, however, was a key design consideration throughout the construction process: The fixtures are constructed of non-formaldehyde composite wood; low-water used fixtures minimize consumption in the restrooms; photo cells shut down electric light-ing when ambient light is sufficient; non-VOC-emitting paint and carpet were used where possible; and 96 percent of construction waste was diverted from landfills and recycled while the store was built. Of course, no REI store would be complete without such amenities as a boot-test station to simulate hiking conditions, a water-filter test basin and a climbing wall. Best of all, the retailer became one of the first U.S. retailers to gain LEED certification for its store.

CLIENT
Recreational Equipment Inc. (REI), Sumner, Wash.
– Laura Rose, design director; Susan Neaton,
project design

DESIGN/ARCHITECTURE
Mithun Architects + Designers + Planners, Seattle
– Chris Dixon, Marty McElveen, Susan McNabb,
Casey Riske, Julia Stahl, Steve Swanson and Paul
Wanzer

GENERAL CONTRACTOR
Howard S. Wright Construction Co., Portland, Ore.

CARPET
Masland Contract, Mobile, Ala.

FIXTURES
REI, Sumner, Wash.

LIGHTING
Villa Lighting, St. Louis

OFFICE SYSTEM FURNITURE
Haworth Inc., Holland, Mich.

PHOTOGRAPHY
Eckert & Eckert, Portland, Ore.

Borders

Louisville, Ky.

SPECIALTY STORE, SALES AREA
10,001 TO 50,000 SQ. FT.

Award of Merit

Borders' prototype redesign eases navigation and puts renewed emphasis on the core product books. A yellow racetrack guides shoppers around the store, which features promotional digital signage, impulse-buy tables, a relocated café, a curved fixturing system, storytime amphitheater, black-and-white images of people reading and Borders' signature red placed along walls and atop fixtures.

CLIENT
Borders Inc., Ann Arbor, Mich. – Tom Robin, director, architecture and construction; Chuck Treber, director, store planning; Padmakar Karve, manager, architectural services; John Newman, manager, store layouts; Dennis Racine, senior manager, store design

DESIGN
Grid2 Intl., New York – Martin Roberts, president; Akka Ma, executive vp, interiors; Betty Chow, vp, graphics; Steven Derwoed, director of projects, interior designer; Lucinda Watt, interior designer

ARCHITECT
URS Corp., Farmington Hills, Mich.

GENERAL CONTRACTOR
Wheeler Building, Bloomfield Hills, Mich.

OUTSIDE DESIGN CONSULTANTS
TES Engineering, Cleveland (mechanical and electrical engineers)

FIXTURES
Huck Store Fixtures, Quincy, Ill.

FLOORING
The Matt Works, Stoughton, Mass.; Durkan, Kennesaw, Ga.

FURNITURE
Falcon, Dandridge, Tenn.

WALLCOVERINGS/MATERIALS
Benjamin Moore Paint Co., Montvale, N.J.; Corian, Wilmington, Del.; LIRI, Torino, Italy; Hakatai, Ashland, Ore.; JM Lynne, Ronkonkoma, N.Y.

NETWORK DIGITAL SIGNAGE
Convergent Media Systems Corp., Atlanta

PHOTOGRAPHY
Gil Stose, Highland, N.C.

American Girl Place

New York

SPECIALTY STORE, SALES AREA
10,001 TO 50,000 SQ. FT.

Award of Merit

The five-story American Girl Place flagship on Fifth Avenue, which includes a theater, café and store, offers the ultimate fancy day out for mothers and daughters. Branding begins with exterior awnings in AG's signature berry red and continues in the details, the store's berry-red carpeting, the foyer's light fixtures with star cutouts and the café's black-and-white striped walls.

CLIENT
American Girl, Middleton, Wis. – Jeff Freeman, senior vp, operations

DESIGN/ARCHITECTURE
Gensler, New York – Walter Hunt, Jr., John Bricker, Tom Rosenkilde, Mark Morton, Dana Jenkins, Kathleen Lepley, Eric Brill, Peg Harris, Xerinna Santa Ana, Laura Bellion, Mieko Oda, Beth Novitsky, Dicie Carlson, Judson Buttner, John Scheffel and Christine Schlilling

GENERAL CONTRACTOR
Vanguard Construction & Development Co. Inc., New York

OUTSIDE DESIGN CONSULTANTS
Hillman DiBernardo & Associates, New York (lighting); FMC Associates, New York (MEP engineer); Thornton-Tomasetti, New York (structural engineer); Cini Little Intl. Inc., New York (food service); Van Deusen & Associates, Livingston, N.J. (vertical transportation); Fisher Dachs Associates, New York (theater design); Cerami & Associates, New York (acoustics); Levy Restaurants, Chicago (food service)

PHOTOGRAPHY
Michelle Litvin, Chicago

World of Disney

New York

SPECIALTY STORE, SALES AREA
OVER 50,000 SQ. FT.

First Place (tie)

There's something for everyone at the World of Disney store on New York's Fifth Avenue, where "retail theater" is taken to new dimensions. For example, the whimsical marquee, curved and designed like a reel of film, and flanking display windows beckon visitors into the indoor theater. Once inside the three-story space, the store offers everything from stuffed animals and other Disney memorabilia to a theater, a place to meet Disney characters and a ticket counter for booking vacations or buying tickets to Disney theme parks.

In the retail area, customization is the order of the day. Little princesses can create their own tiara or jewelry in the courtyard room, where magic mirrors, a chandelier and custom carpet channel Cinderella. Playful visitors can get creative by making their own Mr. Potato Head with such New York icons as Mickey pretzels and pizza, or the Statue of Liberty's torch and crown. Those with a sweet tooth can customize their own candy – gravity-fed or racked – at Goofy's Candy Company, a first-ever Disney installation that features an 8-foot-high Goofy with candy-covered hat and vest. And for those who like to play dress-up, an area with cashmere clothing and the like features mannequins and black-and-white photos that appeal to a more sophisticated sensibility.

CLIENT/DESIGN
Walt Disney Imagineering/Global Retail Store Development,Lake Buena Vista, Fla. – Anthony J. Mancini, senior vp, global retail store development, Walt Disney Imagineering and Walt Disney Parks & Resorts; Johnnie Rush, director, creative development, Walt Disney Imagineering; Tim Johnson, director, project management, Walt Disney Imagineering; Mike Montague, senior project manager, Walt Disney Imagineering; Todd Taylor, manager, store planning, Walt Disney Imagineering; Mark Breller, global portfolio manager, Walt Disney Parks & Resorts; Tom Sheldon, manager, global retail store development production, Walt Disney Imagineering; Jeff Weber, manager, merchandise presentation, Walt Disney Parks & Resorts; Tony D'Orazio, regional manager, merchandise presentation, Walt Disney Parks & Resorts; David MacConnie, merchandise presentation manager, Walt Disney Parks & Resorts

ARCHITECT
Elkus-Manfredi, Boston

GENERAL CONTRACTOR
Turner Interiors, New York

OUTSIDE DESIGN CONSULTANT
ADS Mechanical, New York

FIXTURES
Jasco Industries Inc./MG Concepts, Central Islip, N.Y.; Westco Fixtures, New York

SHELVING
Vira Mfg. Inc., Perth Amboy, N.J.

WINDOW DISPLAY SYSTEMS
ALU, New York

HARDWARE
Reeve Store Equipment Co., Pico Rivera, Calif.

THEMED SPECIALTY FIXTURES, SCULPTURES, WINDOW DISPLAYS
Walt Disney Imagineering/Global Retail Store Development, Lake Buena Vista, Fla.

SPECIALTY BULK CANDY UNITS

Trade Fixtures/New Leaf Designs, Little Rock, Ark.

VISUAL PRESENTATION
Visual Design and Sources, Valrico, Fla.; Chippenhook, Lewisville, Texas; Creative Arts Unlimited, Pinellas Park, Fla.; Trimco, Brooklyn, N.Y.; Designer Plastics Inc., Clearwater, Fla.; Holiday Foliage Inc., San Diego; Christine Taylor Collection, Doylestown, Pa.; Ace Designs, Bristol, Pa.; Southern Exhibit, Orlando; Sunworks Plastics, Clearwater, Fla.

MANNEQUINS
Patina-V, City of Industry, Calif.; Pucci Intl. Ltd., New York; Greneker, Los Angeles

MEDIA AREA SOFTWARE DEVELOPMENT AND SPECIALTY FIXTURES
Best Wave, Scottsdale, Ariz.

PHOTOGRAPHY
Richard Cadan, New York

Bass Pro Shops Outdoor World

Bossier City, La.

SPECIALTY STORE, SALES AREA
OVER 50,000 SQ. FT.

First Place (tie)

*This project also won a
Special Award for innovative
visual merchandising*

Taking a "funky Cajun" approach to their two-story, 110,000-square-foot Bossier City, La., store, designers at Bass Pro Shops used natural materials, faux props and plenty of animal appeal that pepper the store with regional flavor. Plaster walls, local timbers and corrugated tin give the exterior a rustic look, while large windows offer clear sightlines into the themed space. Bold colors and graphics, as well as oversized life-like – and real – props, such as replications of cypress trees, tree houses and stone fireplaces, give visitors the feeling of stepping back into historical times.

To extend the regional flavor, designers invited local hunters and anglers to display their highly unique collections in the space, including collections of lure, duck, elk, whitetail deer and Civil War arms. And visual elements, such as floor carvings of local prehistoric Petra cliffs at the base of the aquarium, hand-painted topographic regional maps on the walls, and black-and-white photos of local huntsman and fisherman, extend the local flavor – and the brand.

CLIENT/DESIGN
Bass Pro Shops Inc., Springfield, Mo. – Tom Jowett, vp, design and development; Tom Gammon, director of construction; Mark Tuttle, director of architecture, project designer; Lenny Clark, senior technical designer; Marek Krukowski, project designer; Glennon Scheid, interior project manager; Dave Geuea, project manager; Monica Matthias, interior project manager of fixtures, signage; Rick Collins, taxidermy; Bruce Teter, retail planning director

ARCHITECT
Creative Ink., Springfield, Mo.

GENERAL CONTRACTOR
Gilbane Building, Houston

LANDSCAPE ARCHITECTS
Spaid Associates, St. Louis

INTERIOR/EXTERIOR DESIGN CONSULTANT
Russ Halley, Springfield, Mo.

IMAGERY CONSULTANT
Marvin Levine, Lipan, Texas

CARPET
Mohawk Carpet, Calhoun, Ga.

FINISHES
Color Brite, Cincinnati

FIXTURES
Bass Pro Fabrication Shop, Nixa, Mo.; Fentress Marine, Largo, Fla.; Lozier, St. Peters, Mo.; TJ Hale, Menomonee Falls, Wis.; White Oak Displays, Manheim, Pa.

FURNITURE
Country Casual, Gaithersburg, Md.; Roadside Rustics, Eureka Springs, Ark.; Rocky Creek, Stephenville, Texas

IMAGERY
Maine Bucket Co., Lewiston, Maine

SIGNAGE AND GRAPHICS
Garage Graphics, Springfield, Mo.; Signs Now, Springfield, Mo.

PHOTOGRAPHY
Douglas K. Hill/Hill Photographics, Snellville, Ga.

CTV Kiosk

**Pearson International
Airport, Toronto**

SHOPPING CENTER KIOSK

First Place

The CTV (Canadian Television) kiosk at Pearson International Airport's newly opened Terminal One is designed with the notion of the city as a media center. Envisioned as a "pebble in the stream" of the airport architecture, the kiosk uses an all-glass enclosure that makes it simultaneously unobtrusive, highly visible and beautifully transparent. Ten-foot-high segments of tempered glass panels are beveled with glass support fins and held together with triangular satin stainless-steel header clips and clear silicone. An innovative transparent film applied to the glass partitions transforms the uppermost glass into a holographic rear-projection screen that appears to be suspended in mid-air.

Below the screens, clear signage directs visitors to the desired magazine subject matter, and a well-organized display system with full-face magazine covers makes the find-and-buy process quick and easy. Customized metal perimeter fixtures of varying heights are self-illuminated and double-sided so that merchandise is visible to customers in the adjacent food court. And illumination is bright and sophisticated, with slim-line track lighting and low-voltage fixtures making the product the hero.

CLIENT
HDS Retail North America, Toronto

DESIGN
Fiorino Design Inc., Toronto – Nella Fiorino, principal designer; Vilija Gacionis and Mike Wilson, designers

GENERAL CONTRACTOR
Sajo Construction, Montreal

AUDIO/VISUAL
Adcom Video Conferencing, Toronto

FIXTURES
Sajo Construction, Montreal

LIGHTING
Lightolier, Toronto; Canlyte, Toronto; Juno Lighting Ltd., Toronto; Technilite Systems Inc., Peterborough, Ont.

SIGNAGE/GRAPHICS
Sunset Neon, Brampton, Ont.

PLASTIC LAMINATE
Nevamar Supplies by McFaddens, Oakville, Ont.; Formica Canada Inc., Toronto

METAL FINISHES
Tiger Drylac Canada Inc., Guelph, Ont.

SOLID SURFACES
McFaddens Hardwood & Hardware Ltd., Oakville, Ont.

PHOTOGRAPHY
David Whittaker, Toronto

Cult Beauty Cosmetics Counter

David Jones, Sydney

SHOPPING CENTER KIOSK

Award of Merit

The new Cult Beauty cosmetics counter creates a unifying element that links seven makeup brands. Arranged in a meandering pattern, the freestanding fixtures feature reflective materials (polished stainless steel and bronze mirror) that create a uniform look, while colors, branding and product displays highlight their individuality.

CLIENT
Trimex, Sydney

DESIGN
Geyer, Sydney – Robyn Lindsey, director; Kirk Lenard, senior designer; Michelle Tarlinton, designer; Georges Boustani, designer

GENERAL CONTRACTOR
Transform Shopfitters, Weatherill Park, New South Wales

PHOTOGRAPHY
Kraig Carlstrom, Sydney

Heavenly Ham Market Café

Gainesville, Fla.

SPECIALTY FOOD COURT OR
COUNTER-SERVICE RESTAURANT

First Place

The redesigned Heavenly Ham Market Café took the fast-casual restaurant from ho-hum to heavenly with a fresh, new look and plenty of personality. Retail merchandising is separated literally and visually from the dining area, with products placed on a dividing island fixture between the two to allow both take-out and dine-in customers to shop.

The right side of the store is product-driven, with easy-to-read signage and colorful, appealing graphics. Warm tiles, earth tones and stained-wood finishes reinforce the down-to-earth atmosphere in the retail and dining areas, while brightly colored, halo-shaped graphic accents play up the heavenly vibe. In the dining area, a sky blue wall with wispy text "clouds" transports diners to higher ground. An oversized halo hangs from the open-truss "night sky" with falling accent lights creating a starry effect. Booths are swathed in blue upholstery that blends in with the walls, and dining tables are topped with message holders in the shape of miniature halos.

CLIENT
Heavenly Ham, Norcross, Ga. – Stan Given, franchisee; Nancy Gibson and Ken Caldwell, senior vps, marketing; Robin Bayless, marketing director

DESIGN
Miller Zell, Atlanta – Keith Curtis, design director, project designer; Victoria Lang, project designer; Debra Yother and Avery Draper, production artists; Devin Nutter, prototype specialist; Robert DeGroff, Jack May and Matt Lukens, design engineers; Jason Isbell, procurement specialist; Tracy Gibson, account executive

ARCHITECT
Don Yanskey, Gainesville, Fla.

GENERAL CONTRACTOR
AMJ Inc., Gainesville, Fla.

GRAPHIC DESIGN CONSULTANT
X3 Creative, Atlanta

FIXTURES
Miller Zell, Atlanta

FLOORING
Traditions in Tile, Alpharetta, Ga.; Witex Laminate Flooring, Atlanta

FURNITURE
Serv-U Kitchen Supplies, Champaign, Ill.; American Base Co., Kansas City, Mo.; Landscape Forms, Kalamazoo, Mich.

FINISHES
Miller Zell, Atlanta; Sherwin-Williams, Cleveland; Benjamin Moore Paint Co., Montvale, N.J.

LAMINATES
Pionite, Auburn, Maine; Formica Corp., Cincinnati; Wilsonart, Temple, Texas

LIGHTING
Tech Lighting, Skokie, Ill.; Peerless Lighting, Berkeley, Calif.; Juno Lighting, Des Plaines, Ill.

SIGNAGE
Miller Zell, Atlanta

PHOTOGRAPHY
Rion Rizzo/Creative Sources Photography, Atlanta

Pick Up Stix

Corona, Calif.

SPECIALTY FOOD COURT/
COUNTER-SERVICE RESTAURANT

Award of Merit

At the redesigned Pick Up Stix, wok-like light fixtures, wall graphics and a new logo featuring chopsticks combine traditional and contemporary Asian elements. Textured bamboo walls separate the dine-in and pick-up counters for more efficient service, while large, colorful menu stands are placed at eye level for easy viewing.

CLIENT
Pick Up Stix, San Clemente, Calif. – Tim Pulido, president/coo; Melanie Bruno-Carbone, executive director of marketing; Lisa Martin, vp of operations; Mark Bunin, director of food quality and sanitation

DESIGN
Chute Gerdeman, Columbus, Ohio – Wendy Johnson, program director; Brian Shafley, creative director; Steve Pottschmidt, design development director; Carmen Costinescu, materials specialist; Santiago Crespo, senior graphic designer; Susan Siewny, graphic production director; Tina Burnham, graphic production coordinator

ARCHITECT
CG Architecture, Columbus, Ohio

OUTSIDE DESIGN CONSULTANTS
Schuler Shook, Minneapolis (lighting); Premier Management Alliance, Tustin, Calif. (project management)

FABRICS
Designtex, New York; Maharam, New York; Architex, Northbrook, Ill.

FIXTURES
Powers, Bolingbrook, Ill.

LAMINATES
Wilsonart, Temple, Texas; Octopus, Toronto; Arpa, Wheeling, Ill.; Nevamar, Odenton, Md.; Formica, Cincinnati

FLOORING
Hamilton Parker, Columbus, Ohio; Flooring Works, Wilkes-Barre, Pa.; Dal-Tile, Dallas

SIGNAGE/GRAPHICS
Permanent Impressions, Huntington Beach, Calif.

LIGHTING
Another Planet, Sonoma County, Calif.; Lumetta, West Warwick, R.I.; Lightolier, Fall River, Mass.

SOLID SURFACE
Corian, Wilmington, Del.; Cambria, Eden Prairie, Minn.

WALLCOVERINGS
Dal-Tile, Dallas; Hamilton Parker, Columbus, Ohio; Surface Style, Columbus, Ohio

PAINTS
Benjamin Moore Paint Co., Montvale, N.J.; Sherwin Williams, Cleveland

FURNITURE
Benchmark Design Group, Jacksonville Beach, Fla.

PHOTOGRAPHY
John Svoboda, Svoboda Studios Inc., Lake Forest, Calif.

Saratoga Springs

Lake Buena Vista, Fla.

SPECIALTY FOOD COURT/
COUNTER-SERVICE RESTAURANT

Award of Merit

This Saratoga Springs beverage/retail venue for Disney's time-share resort guests features an upscale, casual design inspired by an artist's loft. Stained concrete flooring in the food and beverages area adds to the urban feel and makes cleanup easy. Exposed brick, millwork, artful lighting and vibrant banners define the space and scale down the high ceilings.

CLIENT
Walt Disney Parks & Resorts, Lake Buena Vista, Fla.

DESIGN
Walt Disney Imagineering/Global Retail Store Development, Lake Buena Vista, Fla. – Anthony J. Mancini, svp, global retail store development; Tom Sheldon, production (Orlando)

INTERIOR DESIGN
DiLeonardo Interiors, Warwick, R.I.

ARCHITECT
GSB, Oklahoma City, Okla.

GENERAL CONTRACTOR
Hardin Construction, Orlando

OUTSIDE DESIGN CONSULTANTS
HLB Lighting, New York (lighting); Walt Disney Imagineering, Lake Buena Vista, Fla. (graphics)

FIXTURES
Crystolon Inc., Commerce, Calif.; Evans Equipment, Apopka, Fla.; Westco, New York

FOOD RESTAURANT/SUPPLIES
Hubert Co., Cincinnati

METAL MANUFACTURER
S&B Metal, Lakeland, Fla.

SIGNAGE AND GRAPHICS
Graphics/DWI, Lake Buena Vista, Fla.

VISUAL MERCHANDISING/PROPS
Revivals, Orlando; SunWorks Plastics, Clearwater, Fla.; Themes & Concepts, Orlando

PHOTOGRAPHY
Lee McKee, Orlando

Bellanotte

Minneapolis

SIT-DOWN RESTAURANT

First Place

To create a "beautiful night" out for diners, designers of the Bella-notte restaurant mixed traditional Tuscan-style elements with modern touches, and used a palette of warm and color-infused tones to offer a bright, cozy respite from the cold Minneapolis winters. Most of the 10,000-square-foot space is taken up by a main bar off the entrance, a second bar in the main dining room and a lounge with private bar and dining room. The latter accommodates large crowds arriving after events at the nearby Target Center.

The emphasis on clean lines is evident throughout the space in such details as a freestanding glass-enclosed wine tower in the bar area; floor-to-ceiling red oak panels with protruding square pendants in natural mica; and a glowing amber onyx stone countertop at the main bar. Other focal elements add warmth and modernity, including a central working stone and glass fire pit in the octagonal dining room, a series of color-changing acrylic panels that divide the space in the main dining room and color-changing LEDs that illuminate the entire space. But traditional Tuscan flair pervades the space in bronze and sheer drapes over the perimeter windows, Venetian-stuccoed walls and sof-fits and the combination of wenge-wood millwork and flooring, light-colored upholstered banquettes and a palette of beiges and oranges.

CLIENT
David Koch and Kam Talebi, Minneapolis

DESIGN/ARCHITECTURE
Echeverria Design Group Inc., Coral Gables, Fla. – Mario Echeverria, president; John Naranjo, project senior designer; Robert Dominguez, project manager

GENERAL CONTRACTOR
Diversified Construction, St. Louis Park, Minn.

LIGHTING
Florida Architecture Lighting, Pompano Beach, Fla.; Stephane Dagani, New York

KITCHEN CONSULTANTS
Premier Restaurant Equipment, Minneapolis

FURNITURE
The La Sala Group, Hollywood, Fla.

CUSTOM MILLWORK
Vision Woodworking, Fridley, Minn.

SOUND SYSTEM CONSULTANT
Sound Stage Systems, North Haven, Conn.

SIGNAGE
Signcrafters, Fridley, Minn.

PHOTOGRAPHY
Douglas Reid Fogelson Photography, Chicago

Mariposa

**Neiman Marcus,
Fashion Island,
Newport Beach, Calif.**

SIT-DOWN RESTAURANT

Award of Merit

The 4320-square-foot Mariposa exudes an elegant-but-casual air that targets upscale left-coast customers looking to dine after a day of shopping. The well-appointed entry opens up to the main dining area, which features large framed mirrors, custom-designed rugs and a wall of windows that highlight a garden terrace with ocean views and outdoor seating.

CLIENT
Neiman Marcus, Dallas – Wayne Hussey, senior vp; Cliff Suen, vp; Collette Ventrone, vp; Victor Molaschi, senior project manager; Chris Lebamoff, director; Julia McCullough, director; Steve Vanlandingham, project manager; Megan Hermann, designer

DESIGN
Charles Sparks + Company, Westchester, Ill. – Charles Sparks, president and ceo; Donald Stone, evp, account manager; David Koe, senior creative designer; Stephen Prosser, account coordinator; Fred Wiedenbeck, director, resource studio; Rachel Mikolajczyk, designer, resource studio

ARCHITECT
AP&T, Pasadena, Calif.

GENERAL CONTRACTOR
Swinerton Builders, Newport Beach, Calif.

OUTSIDE DESIGN CONSULTANTS
Integrated Lighting Concepts, Thousand Oaks, Calif.; KLR Associates, Cincinnati

FLOORING
Bentley/Prince Street, Chicago; Mid America Tile, Mundelein, Ill.; Pacific Looms, Irvine, Calif.

COUNTERTOP
Mid America Tile, Mundelein, Ill.

FABRICS
Spinney Beck, Chicago; ICF Group, Chicago; Great Plains, Chicago; David Sutherland, Dallas

FURNITURE
Niedermaier, Chicago; Scott & Cooner, Dallas; David Sutherland, Dallas; Andreu World America Inc., Gardner, Mass.

LIGHTING
Boyd, Chicago; New Metalcrafts, Chicago

MILLWORK
Suss Woodcraft, Montreal

SPECIAL PLASTER FINISH
Raymond Interiors, Orange, Calif.

WOOD FINISH
R.S. Bacon Veneer, Hillside, Ill.

PHOTOGRAPHY
Charlie Mayer, Oak Park, Ill.

TerraVida
Coffee Concept

Shoreline, Wash.

SPECIALTY FOOD SHOP

First Place

When developing the 400-square-foot prototype for TerraVida, a new retail coffee concept in Seattle, the retailer wanted to differentiate itself from big-name competitors with a concept that focuses on the small coffee bean grower, the community and, as the name suggests, a strong connection between earth and life. A team of interior and graphic designers worked with a branding consultant and the Haggen team (owners of TerraVida) to come up with a colorful, organic, graphic-driven prototype space at the TOP Foods store in Shoreline, Wash.

The earthy design features clay-colored walls that allow for an expression of the wood-surrounded "fossils" that penetrate the surface and display found objects of modern discoveries. "Life" is conveyed through curving layers of brightly colored materials that explain the functions involved in creating each cup of coffee. And, at the entrance, a funnel-shaped focal element, or "totem," graphically displays Earth on one half and Life on the other, telling the TerraVida story.

CLIENT
Haggen Inc., Bellingham, Wash.

DESIGN/ARCHITECTURE
GGLO, Seattle – Bill Gaylord, principal-in-charge; Jennifer Thuma, project designer/project manager; Michelle Mahaney, project designer; Julie Petri and Kimberly Frank, designers

GENERAL CONTRACTOR
T.W. Clark, Spokane, Wash.

PACKAGING AND GRAPHIC DESIGN
Hornall Anderson Design Works, Seattle

CUSTOM CASEWORK/FIXTURES
OB Williams Co., Seattle

SURFACES
DuPont, Wilmington, Del.; Interlam, Claudville, Va.; 3form, Salt Lake City; Nevamar, Odenton, Md.; Pionite, Shelton, Conn.; ICI Paints, Winter Park, Fla.; Forbo USA, Hazleton, Pa.

LIGHTING
Bruck Lighting Systems, Costa Mesa, Calif.; Edison Price Lighting, Long Island City, N.Y.; Ardee Lighting, Shelby, N.C.; Peerless Lighting, Berkeley, Calif.; Columbia Lighting, Bristol, Pa.; Lithonia Lighting, Conyers, Ga.

PHOTOGRAPHY
Steve Keating Photography, Port Orchard, Wash.

Earth, meet Life. Life, me

Maxi Markt

Bruck, Austria

SUPERMARKET

First Place

A new concept for Maxi Markt, the large-scale Austrian grocery retailer sells groceries, as well as some limited lines of apparel, toys and home goods. The focus is on easy and immediate access to products – for customers stocking up in remote, even hostile regions in central Europe – and creating a feeling of approachability despite the store's vast size. To increase visibility from the nearby mountains, the store's exterior retains the familiar 1970s logo and features a neon "just landed" structure that adds dramatic visual impact.

Once inside the 52,000-square-foot retail shed, designers created a "forced flow" traffic pattern that ensures customers pass by every section before checking out and leaving. In the kids' section, an interactive Lego castle encourages young customers to shop and play; sports and fashion are linked by a ski ramp; and a bistro mimics an apres-ski environment at a Tyrolean resort. Industrial high-bay lamps flood the entire space with light, and a series of zones – events, tastings or promotions – marked by perimeter super graphics give customers a surprise at every turn.

CLIENT
Interspar Group, Salzburg, Austria – Marcus Wild, Marcus Kaiser and Herr Shrenk, management board
DESIGN
JHP Design, London – Steve Collis, strategy director ; Raj Wilkinson, creative director; David Rook, associate design director; Heike Brandt, designer; Darren Scott, communications director
ARCHITECT
ATP Architekten und Ingenieure, Innsbruck, Austria
GENERAL CONTRACTOR
Linde Ag, Wiesbaden, Germany
LIGHTING
Bartenbach Lichtlabor GmbH, Aldrans, Austria
PHOTOGRAPHY
SLR Photography, London

Home
Economist
Market

Charlotte, N.C.

SUPERMARKET

Award of Merit

A new company name, logo, fixturing system and interior design mark the revamped Home Economist Market, an organic grocery retailer. Wood flooring, exposed ceiling trusses and murals on rough canvases contribute to the natural, organically grown feel. And progressive wall colors, low-profile shelving and unobtrusive signage make navigation easy and intuitive for shoppers.

CLIENT
Home Economist Market, Charlotte, N.C. – Tom Zerbinos, president of retail operations; Dick Harrell

DESIGN/ARCHITECTURE
Little Diversified Architectural Consulting, Charlotte, N.C. – Tim Morrison, principal-in-charge; Daniel Montaño, design director; Mohammad Ismail, project manager; Paige Brice, interior designer; Phillip Petty, environmental graphic designer; John Ellis, job captain

GENERAL CONTRACTOR
Heard Ratzlaff Construction, Charlotte, N.C.

OUTSIDE DESIGN CONSULTANTS
Bliss Fasman Inc., New York (lighting); Bowers Consulting, Red Lion, Pa. (mechanical engineers); WGPM Inc., Charlotte, N.C. (structural engineers); Sturgill Engineering, Lexington, N.C. (electrical engineers); C.E. Holt Equipment Co., Charlotte, N.C. (refrigeration)

FLOORING
Amtico Intl., Atlanta

LIGHTING
Maddux Lighting, Greensboro, N.C.

SIGNAGE AND GRAPHICS
Visual Impressions, Charlotte, N.C.; Plastex Fabrication, Charlotte, N.C.; Casco, Kannapolis, N.C.

PHOTOGRAPHY
Jeffrey Clare, Charlotte, N.C.

BULK FOODS

SNACK MIXES · GRAINS · NUTS · DRIED FRUITS

YOGURT / CAROB CANDY

COFFEE & JUICE

FRESH JUICE

GRAB & GO

MEALS TO GO

DELI

Sheetz Convenience Restaurant

Altoona, Pa.

CONVENIENCE STORE

First Place

When it started out 50 years ago, Sheetz was a gas station. Today, Sheetz is a $2 billion convenience store chain with 300 locations. But despite its success, the retailer wanted to put more emphasis on food items, to change the venue from being a "gas station with food" to a "restaurant with fuel." To this end, the 10,000-square-foot prototype devotes most of its space to food service, including made-to-order salads, pizza and coffee, with a well-appointed dining area that has a contemporary, sophisticated feel.

Touchscreen ordering kiosks at an order island allow customers to view the selection, while also separating the food-ordering element from the food itself. The comprehensive environmental graphics program reinforces the Sheetz brand by incorporating its trademark colors (red and green), a clear, readable typeface, curvilinear design, and fun references to the brand (i.e., "Shmuffinz"). Wood and tile floors, as well as tile backsplashes and large, pendant lights, give the space a restaurant feel. Outside, the red brick, residential-style exterior features bright awnings, umbrella table seating and a two-story clerestory entrance that extend Sheetz's new focus.

CLIENT
Sheetz Inc., Altoona, Pa. – Steve Sheetz, board chairman; Stan Sheetz, president, ceo; Louis Sheetz, executive vp, marketing; Joe M. Sheetz, vp, store development; Joe S. Sheetz, executive vp, finance; W. Daniel McMahon, executive vp, operations; Bill Reilly, executive vp, sales and marketing; Travis Sheetz, vp, regional manager of operations; Rick Cyman, vp, store development; John Moulton, director of store systems; Colleen Devorris, brand development; Ieva Allison, research; Tammy Dunkley, advertising manager

DESIGN
Chute Gerdeman Inc., Columbus, Ohio – Elle Chute, principal; Denny Gerdeman, principal; Wendy Johnson, program director/environments; Eric Kuhn, creative director/environments; Ann Dury, environments designer; Steve Pottschmidt, design development director; Carmen Costinescu, materials specialist; Mindi Trank, program director/graphics; Eric Daniel, creative director/graphics; Santiago Crespo, senior graphic designer; Steve Boreman, Chad Witzel and Brad Egnor, graphic designers; Susan Siewny, graphic production director; Tina Burnham, graphic production coordinator

ARCHITECT
CG Architecture, Columbus, Ohio

GENERAL CONTRACTOR
Sheetz Inc., Altoona, Pa.

CEILING
Benjamin Moore Paint Co., Montvale, N.J.; Sherwin-Williams, Cleveland

FLOORING
Hamilton Parker, Columbus, Ohio; Flooring Works, Wilkes-Barre, Pa.; Dal-Tile, Dallas; Endicott, Fairbury, Neb.; Grand Entrance, Gaithersburg, Md.

SIGNAGE/GRAPHICS
LSI Industries, Canton, Ohio; Blair Sign Co., Altoona, Pa.; Allure Fusion Media, Atlanta; Florida Plastics, Orlando; Radiant Technologies, Atlanta

LIGHTING
Hite Co., Altoona, Pa.; Schuler Shook, Minneapolis

LAMINATES
Wilsonart, Temple, Texas; Octopus, Toronto; Arpa, Chicago; Nevamar, Odenton, Md.; Formica, Cincinnati

SOLID SURFACE
Corian, Wilmington, Del.; Cambria, Eden Prairie, Minn.; Decorative Plastic; 3form, Salt Lake City

POWDERCOATS
Prismatic Powders, White City, Ore.

WALLCOVERINGS
Johnsonite, Chagrin Falls, Ohio; Dal-Tile, Dallas; Endicott, Fairbury, Neb.; Hamilton Parker, Columbus, Ohio; United States Ceramics, East Sparta, Ohio; Surface Style, Columbus, Ohio; Benjamin Moore Paint Co., Montvale, N.J.; Sherwin-Williams, Cleveland

FIXTURES
Florian Cabinets, Pittsburgh; Ken's Graphics, Medina, Ohio; Royston, LLC, Jasper, Ga.

FURNITURE
Benchmark Design Group, Jacksonville Beach, Fla.

FABRICS
Designtex, New York; Maharam, Hauppauge, N.Y.; Architex, Northbrook, Ill.

ROOFING
Pac-Clad, Elk Grove Village, Ill.

PHOTOGRAPHY
Mark Steele, Columbus, Ohio

Pin-Up Bowl

St. Louis

ENTERTAINMENT FACILITY

First Place

At this St. Louis bowling alley/martini lounge, designers were challenged with creating a popular destination point for fun and relaxation that doesn't imitate any one style or era. Inspired by classic art deco elements, but with modern graphics and materials, the overall look is at once familiar and entirely unique. The 10-by-26-foot exterior neon sign features two imaginary pin-up characters – Camille and Antonio – alongside a bowling ball, a pair of bowling pins and martini glasses.

Inside, a bar and adjacent red wrap-around banquettes offer a cozy place to relax and sip martinis between games. Here, a table with bowling-pin legs and the owner's personal collection of vintage pin-up posters on the walls reinforce the venue's dual theme. Wood display fixtures are a neutral backdrop for the colorful bowling balls, pool-table cues, shoes and other related merchandise – some of which feature Camille and Antonio. Velvet draperies add sophistication to the space, while high-tech elements, such as large-format video displays, plasma screens, a digital jukebox and a first-class sound system, ensure a good time for a hip, contemporary crowd.

CLIENT
Joe Edwards, St. Louis

DESIGN/ARCHITECTURE
Kiku Obata & Co., St. Louis – Kiku Obata, Kevin Flynn, Dennis Hyland, Rich Nelson, Eleanor Safe, Jef Ebers, Mel Lim-Keylon, Lisa Bollmann, Carole Jerome, Todd Owyoung and Amy Knopf

GENERAL CONTRACTOR
ISC Contracting, St. Louis

STRUCTURAL ENGINEERING
KPFF Consulting Engineers, St. Louis

MECHANICAL, ELECTRICAL, PLUMBING, FIRE PROTECTION, CIVIL ENGINEERING
William Tao & Associates, St. Louis

ILLUSTRATOR
Joe Keylon, San Diego

LIGHTING
Lithonia Lighting, Conyers, Ga.; Eureka, Toronto; Halo Lighting, Peachtree City, Ga.; Ardee Lighting, Shelby, N.C.; Focal Point, Chicago; Metalux, Houston; Tech Lighting, Skokie, Ill.

FURNITURE FABRIC
Designtex, New York

DRAPERIES
Woodart Contract LLC, St. Louis

CARPET
Lees Carpet, Greensboro, N.C.

MILLWORK
Woodbyrne, St. Louis

CEILING TILE
US Gypsum, Chicago

TILE
Crossville, Crossville, Tenn.; US Ceramic Tile Co., East Sparta, Ohio

SIGNAGE/GRAPHICS
Engraphix, St. Louis

AUDIO
Technical Productions Inc., St. Louis

PHOTOGRAPHY
Jon Miller, Chicago

MAPLE LEAF
LOUNGE
SALON
FEUILLE D'ÉRABLE

STAR ALLIANCE ✦ | GOLD

Air Canada Maple Leaf Lounge

Pearson International Airport, Toronto

SERVICE RETAILER

First Place

This project also won a Special Award for innovative architecture

Although Air Canada's lounges already were popular among its business travelers, the airline wanted to update the spaces to create an expansive, welcoming environment that would appeal to a diverse group of elite travelers, including families, men and women, build brand equity; and lead to new sponsorship revenue streams. The design firm and architects drafted a plan, got approval and then went back to the drawing board after a new location was contracted for and the budget was cut by 30 percent. No matter. The 22,000-square-foot lounge at Toronto's Pearson International Airport is a cohesive exercise in modern design and luxury.

A red lacquer wall and steel screen in the lobby frames a long view of the lounge beyond. Once inside, a series of circulation loops define smaller destination areas for refreshments, entertainment and business. A panoramic window signifies one path, while a suspended canopy marks the other. Enclosed by low walnut and glass walls, the raised terrace occupies ample interior space to maximize panoramic exterior views. And throughout the space, a sophisticated materials palette that includes granite, stained walnut, zebra and sycamore wood, clear and sandblasted glass and dark-brown mosaic glass tiles extends the first-class feel.

CLIENT
Air Canada, Toronto – Nathalie Filippetti

DESIGN
II BY IV Design Associates Inc., Toronto – Dan Menchions, Keith Rushbrook

ARCHITECT
Kuwabara Payne McKenna Blumberg Architects, Toronto

GENERAL CONTRACTOR
Urbacon Ltd., Toronto

ELECTRICAL ENGINEER
Plan Group, Toronto

MECHANICAL ENGINEER
Sayers Associates, Mississauga, Ont.

LIGHTING DESIGN
Suzanna Powadiuk, Toronto

FLOORING
Interface, Toronto; Ciot Marble & Granite, Concord, Ont.; Olympia Tile, Toronto; The Sullivan Source, Toronto

GLASS
Vast Interiors, Concord, Ont.; Barber Glass, Guelph, Ont.; PPG Industries, Pittsburgh

SURFACES
Evolve Architectural Coatings, Toronto; Ciot Marble & Tile, Concord, Ont.; General Woods and Veneers, Mississauga, Ont.; ICI Paints, Toronto

WINDOW TREATMENT FABRIC
Maharam, Toronto

LIGHTING
Eurolite, Toronto; Sistemalux, Toronto; Artemide, Toronto

SOLAR SHADES
Solarfective Products, Toronto

FURNITURE
Nienkamper, Toronto; Teknion, Toronto; Herman Miller, Toronto

PHOTOGRAPHY
David Whittaker, Toronto

Seven Seventeen Credit Union

Hubbard, Ohio

SERVICE RETAILER

Award of Merit

The bank's colorful, graphically driven design focuses on eliminating barriers between tellers and customers. In the personalized financial services area, half-high partitions provide intimacy but allow sightlines to the entrance. Online transactions take place at computer workstations with complimentary refreshments. And transitional flooring and visual merchandising mark the teller service station.

CLIENT
Seven Seventeen Credit Union, Warren, Ohio – Cheryl D'Amore, vp, administrative services; Lori Lambert, space planning and interiors facilitator

DESIGN
TRIAD Architects, Columbus, Ohio – Peter Macrae, president, principal-in-charge; YuFung Tim Lai, environmental brand designer

GENERAL CONTRACTOR
The Kreidler Construction Co., Poland, Ohio

ARCHITECT/CIVIL AND STRUCTURAL ENGINEERS
Baker Bednar & Associates, Warren, Ohio

OUTSIDE DESIGN CONSULTANTS
Steel Valley Engineering, Youngstown, Ohio (plumbing, mechanical and electrical engineer); Ideal Image Inc., Englewood, Ohio (fixtures/graphics); Wiedenbach-Brown Co. Inc., Columbus, Ohio (lighting); De La Rue, Basingstoke, U.K. (financial services equipment design/build)

STOREFRONT
YKK AP America Inc., Austell, Ga.

FLOORING
In-Vision Carpet Systems, Dalton, Ga.; Blue Ridge, Ellijay, Ga.; Bentley, City of Industry, Calif.; Pergo, Trelleborg, Sweden; Mannington, Calhoun, Ga.

PAINT
Sherwin-Williams, Cleveland

HARDWARE
Schlage, Crystal Lake, Ill.; LCN Closers, Mountain Home, Ark.; Hager, St. Louis; Trimco, Los Angeles

PLASTIC LAMINATES
Wilsonart, Temple, Texas; Formica, Cincinnati

FIXTURE HARDWARE
Baer Supply Co., Columbus, Ohio; Häfele, Archdale, N.C.; Doug Mockett & Co., Manhattan Beach, Calif.

SIGNAGE/GRAPHICS
Photo Lab Inc., Cincinnati; Fast Signs, Hubert Heights, Ohio

LIGHTING
Lithonia Lighting, Conyers, Ga.; Davis/Muller, Pawtucket, R.I.; Con-Tech, Northbrook, Ill.; Gotham, Conyers, Ga.; Lightech, South Laguna, Calif.; LSI Industries Inc., Cincinnati; Exitronix, Phoenix; Peerless Lighting, Berkeley, Calif.

PHOTOGRAPHY
John Evan, J.E. Evans Photography, Galena, Ohio

Got
big?
plans

Seven Seventeen makes
home improvements
affordable.   **Apply today!**

Get a Home Equity Line of Credit
as low as
3.75%

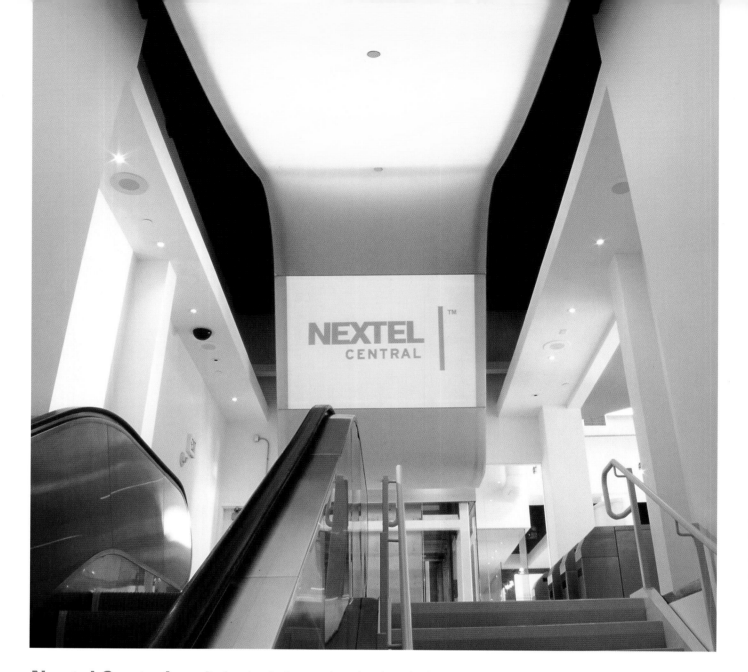

Nextel Central

Las Vegas

MANUFACTURER'S SHOWROOM

First Place

Designed as both a transit station along the Las Vegas Monorail route and a showcase for the wireless brand's integrated services, the 15,000-square-foot Nextel Central offers a little something for everyone. A unifying architectural feature – the Ribbon – snakes through the space and integrates five distinct areas: the entry lobby and welcome desk, the Center of Excellence and wireless VIP lounge, the concierge and business solutions center, exhibition space and a retail store. A swooping ceiling, theatrical lighting and video technology add to the space's experiential feel. Here, travelers can view Nextel's services and products at 3-D interactive video displays, check e-mail in the wireless lounge, or enjoy views of the Las Vegas Strip on the open-air balcony.

CLIENT
Nextel Telecommunications, Reston, Va. – Miguel Lecuona

DESIGN/ARCHITECTURE
Gensler of Nevada, Las Vegas – Marty Borko, project principal; J.F. Finn, project director; Carolina Tombolesi, project manager; Irwin Miller, project designer; Christian Daniels, graphic designer; Banning Rowles, brand and exhibit designer; Hector Ayala, project architect; James Jones, architect; Hui-Ling Hsieh, project interior designer; Darlene Urgola, architecture designer

GENERAL CONTRACTOR
Marnell Corrao Associates, Las Vegas

OUTSIDE DESIGN CONSULTANTS
Edwards Technologies Inc., Los Angeles; Mindshare, New York; Syska Hennessey Group Inc., Las Vegas; REZN 8, Los Angeles; Horton Lees Brogden Lighting Design, Los Angeles; Brand Architecture Intl., New York; Southland Industries, Las Vegas; Rees Masilionis Turley Architecture, Kansas City, Mo.; Rolf Jensen & Associates, Las Vegas

CEILING
Newmant Ceilings, Huntington, N.Y.

LIGHTING
Color Kinetics, Boston; Translite Sonoma, Sonoma, Calif.; Valley Lighting, Linthicum, Md.

SURFACES
Knoll Industries, Santa Monica, Calif.; Shaw Carpet, Cypress, Calif.

MILLWORK
Alexander Mfg. Inc., Portland, Ore.

SIGNAGE
Yesco, Las Vegas

FIXTURES
Wisconsin Built, Deerfield, Wis.

FURNITURE
ICF Group, Santa Monica, Calif.; Martin Brattrud, Gardena, Calif.

GLAZING
Aheinaman Contract Glazing, Las Vegas

VIDEO
Daktronics, San Diego

PHOTOGRAPHY
Eric Laignel, New York

Michael Jordan Asia Tour

Beijing; Hong Kong; Taipei; Tokyo

MANUFACTURER'S SHOWROOM

Award of Merit

This traveling exhibit for Nike's Jordan division was designed as a public showroom and total-immersion brand experience. Features included a 30-foot image of Jordan's wing span; a "futures" wall with monitors and LED display; a video lounge with plasma screens, leather booths and Team Jordan athletes; a curved marble runway; and a graphic wall detailing the brand's history.

CLIENT
Nike Inc., Beaverton, Ore. – Keith Crawford, creative director, Brand Jordan; Michael Delaney, art director, Nike Asia/Pacific; Joon Chattigre, copywriter, Nike Inc.

DESIGN
Twenty Four•Seven Inc., Portland, Ore. – Craig Wollen, vp, creative services; Rebecca Huston, design director; Cody Barnickel, graphic design; Wade Wheeler, design engineer; Shane Fletcher, design engineers

PHOTOGRAPHY
Nike Inc., Beaverton, Ore.

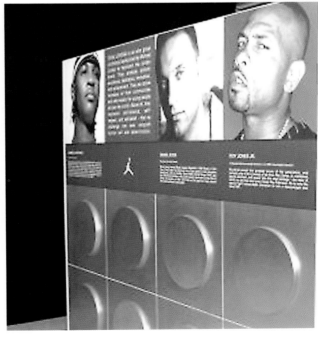

Walker Zanger Manhattan Showroom

New York

MANUFACTURER'S SHOWROOM

Award of Merit

It's a material world at Walker Zanger's well-appointed 6200-square-foot showroom. Limestone signage complements the landmark building's façade, while stained wood, limestone and a glass mosaic lend luxe to the entryway. Inside, mosaics, handmade ceramics, stone and tile are displayed in situ, including a wine cellar that shows the products' possibilities.

CLIENT
Walker Zanger, Mt. Vernon, N.Y. – Leon Zanger, owner

DESIGN
Walker Zanger Facilities Design, Sylmar, Calif. – Kim Bernard, director; Lisa Salloux, senior designer; Kim McOwan, senior designer; Jerry Newman, architect; Jessica Cerny, CAD; George Sisneros, installations

ARCHITECT
Ronnette Riley Architect, New York

GENERAL CONTRACTOR
Bronx Builders, New York

OUTSIDE DESIGN CONSULTANT
Gotham Light and Power, East Hampton, N.Y. (lighting)

STONE
Fordham Marble Co., Stamford, Conn.; Mosaic Creation, Newark, N.J.; Jim-Mar Marble and Granite, Deerpark, N.Y.; Dimensional Tile & Stone, New Rochelle, N.Y.

FIXTURES
Cascade Metal Design, Chatsworth, Calif.; Eagle Woodworking, Long Island City, N.Y.; Gianelli Cabinets, Northridge, Calif.

FAUX FINISHES
The Classic Finish, New York

PHOTOGRAPHY
Dub Rogers Photography, New York

Nalley Lexus Galleria

Smyrna, Ga.

AUTO DEALERSHIPS

First Place

In keeping with the notion of surprising and pampering its customers, Lexus wanted a dramatic, luxurious, full-service environment for its Smyrna, Ga., dealership. The Nalley Lexus Galleria doesn't disappoint. A carefully designed traffic pattern takes Lexus owners, and potential buyers, through a three-step process designed to help them learn about, buy and maintain the Lexus of their dreams.

At the entrance, a pale granite porcelain floor, concierge desk of black marble and custom-finished cherry maple, circular track lighting and hanging art glass fixtures set the high-end tone. Inside the 92,000-square-foot showroom theater, 38-foot-high glass walls rimmed in steel and topped with concrete add to the dramatic feel. To extend the brand experience, designers installed two 15-by-52-foot billboards and an 11-by-17-foot video screen that shows the product on the road.

In the showroom, Lexus models are displayed in charcoal gray, glass-tile circles surrounded by black river-stone borders. In the retail arena, a featured car and custom duotone lifestyle graphics complement the Lexus merchandise. And no luxury car-shopping experience would be complete without coffee. So Café Lexus offers customers a complimentary beverage break, so they can relax and decide on the right shade of chartreuse over a cappuccino.

CLIENT
Nalley Automotive Group, Atlanta – Asbury Automotive, New York

DESIGN
Praxis3 P.C., Atlanta – Craig James, principal
R. Sway Associates, Roswell, Ga. – Russell Sway, president
Ken Walker, New York

ARCHITECT
Praxis3 P.C., Atlanta

GENERAL CONTRACTOR
Choate Construction Co., Atlanta

MECHANICAL ENGINEER
MEHA, Norcross, Ga.

CIVIL ENGINEER
Matrix Development Group, Marietta, Ga.

STRUCTURAL ENGINEER
Estes Shields Engineering, Atlanta

LIGHTING CONSULTANT
Deco Lighting Design, Ann Arbor, Mich.

FURNITURE CONSULTANT
Office Images, Roswell, Ga.

COFFEE SERVICES CONSULTANT
Starbucks Inc. Food Services, Seattle

ARCHITECTURAL SIGNAGE
MC Signs, Tampa, Fla.

GRAPHICS PRODUCTION
Meteor, Atlanta

PROJECTION SYSTEMS
Barco Projection Systems, Kuurne, Belgium

PRECAST CONCRETE
Metromont Prestress Co., Greenville, S.C.

STRUCTURAL STEEL
Brown Steel, Newman, Ga.

GLASS
Arch Aluminum & Glass Co., Tamarc, Fla.; Viracon, Owatonna, Minn.; Sumiglass, Fenton Harbor, Mich.

SKYLIGHTS
Wasco Products Inc., Sanford, Maine

ALUMINUM COMPOSITE METAL PANELS
Reynolds Architectural Products, Richmond, Va.

FIREPLACE
Lennox Hearth Products, Orange, Calif.

DOORS
Clopay Building Products Co., Cincinnati; Algoma Hardwoods, Inc., Algoma, Wis.

FURNITURE
Loewenstein, Pompano Beach, Fla.; Paoli, Paoli, Ind.; Haworth, Holland, Mich.; Martin/Brattrud Inc., Gardena, Calif.; David Edwards, Baltimore; Keilhauser Industries Ltd., Scarborough, Ont.; Bernhardt Furniture Co., Lenoir, N.C.

FABRICS
Valley Forge Fabrics Inc., Pompano Beach, Fla.; Sina Pearson Textiles NYC, New York

FIXTURES
Ballistic Studios, Lawrenceville, Ga.; Opto Intl., Chicago; Reeve Store Equipment Co., Pico Rivera, Calif.; Häfele America, Archdale, N.C.

WALLCOVERINGS
Designtex, New York; MDC Wallcoverings, Elk Grove Village, Ill.; Genesys Wallcovering, Atlanta; J. Josephson, New York; Wolf Gordon, New York; JM Lynne, New York

CEILINGS/WALLBASES
Armstrong World Industries, Lancaster, Pa.

FLOOR/WALL TILE
Crossville Ceramics, Crossville, Tenn.; Dal-Tile, Dallas

CARPET
Masland Carpets, Mobile, Ala.

SURFACES
Stone Source, New York; Nevamar, Odenton, Md.; Dupont, Wilmington, Del.

LIGHTING
LSI Lighting Systems, Cincinnati; Spalding, Cincinnati; Hydrel, Sylmar, Calif.; RBF Commercial, Dallas; Prescolite Inc., Spartanburg, S.C.; Translite Sonoma, Sonoma, Calif.; Hubbell Inc., Christiansburg, Va.; Lightolier, Fall River, Mass.; Winona Lighting, Winona, Minn.; Columbia Lighting, Bristol, Pa.; Primus Lighting, El Monte, Calif.

ESPRESSO EQUIPMENT
Starbucks Coffee Inc., Food Services Div., Seattle

PHOTOGRAPHY
Reis Birdwhistell, Atlanta

JM Lexus

Margate, Fla.

AUTO DEALERSHIPS

Award of Merit

To join the east and west ends of this Lexus showroom, designers created a rotunda, complete with bistro and lounge, where customers can relax and actually enjoy the car-buying experience. Light, neutral colors and dramatic lighting highlight the displays, while custom stained woods and residential finishes make it feel like an extension of a Lexus customer's well-appointed home.

CLIENT
JM Family Enterprises, Margate, Fla. – Jim Perry, manager of design and construction; Rick Jorden, director of design

DESIGN/ARCHITECTURE
Pavlik Design Team, Ft. Lauderdale, Fla. – R.J. Pavlik, president/ceo; Placido Herrera, partner; Luis Valladares, partner; Todd Perrodine, director of architecture; Jae Kyung Kim, project manager; Mario Duclos, project managers; Tiera Lindsey, project designer

GENERAL CONTRACTOR
Dana B. Kenyon Co., Jacksonville, Fla.

FLOORING
Crossville Tile, Crossville, Tenn.; Bentley-Prince Street Carpet, City of Industry, Calif.

WALLCOVERINGS
Benjamin Moore Paint Co., Montvale, N.J.; Innovations in Wallcovering, New York

FURNITURE
Steelcase, Grand Rapids, Mich.; HBF Furniture, Hickory, N.C.; David Edward, Baltimore; Keilhauer, Toronto

CUSTOM MILLWORK
Quantum Fine Casework, Ft. Lauderdale, Fla.

LIGHTING
Boyd Lighting Co., San Francisco

PHOTOGRAPHY
Dana Hoff, North Palm Beach, Fla.

Elmhurst Toyota

Elmhurst, Ill.

AUTO DEALERSHIPS

Award of Merit

Designers brought the outdoors in to this 27,800-square-foot show-room by installing a faux streetscape down the center-with streetlights, brick pavers, sidewalks and even storefronts. A café area, big-screen theater and children's playground make up the waiting area, while a construction zone defines the retail space.

CLIENT
Elmhurst Toyota, Elmhurst, Ill. – Kurt Schiele, owner

DESIGN/ARCHITECTURE
Ideation Studio Inc., Chicago – Jennifer Nemec, principal

ARCHITECT
Balay Architects Inc., Indianapolis

CARPETING
Lees Commercial Carpet, Kennesaw, Ga.

CEILING SYSTEM
Chicago Metallic Corp., Chicago; Celotex, Tampa

FLOORING
Armstrong World Industries, Lancaster, Pa.; Atmosphere Rubber Flooring, Minneapolis; Crossville Ceramics, Crossville, Tenn.; Emil/Virginia Tile Co., Woodale, Ill.; Impo Glaztiels Inc., Elk Grove Village, Ill.; Stone Design, Glendale Heights, Ill.

FURNITURE
IntraSpace, Oak Park, Ill.

LIGHTING
Abolite, Cincinnati ; Bartco Lighting, Huntington Beach, Calif.; Contrast Lighting, Quebec City, Que.; Hilite/RLM, Chino, Calif.; Juno Lighting, Des Plaines, Ill.; King Luminaire, Jefferson, Ohio; Lightolier, Fall River, Mass.; LiteLab, Buffalo, N.Y.; SistemaLux, Roseville, Calif.; Toki-star Lighting Systems, Anaheim, Calif.; Translite Sonoma, Sonoma, Calif.

METAL LAMINATES
Chemetal, Wheeling, Ill.

PAINTS
ICI/Glidden Paints, Avon Lake, Ohio

PLASTIC LAMINATES
Formica, Cincinnati; Advanced Technology Plastics, Wheeling, Ill.; ARPA, Wheeling, Ill.; Pionite, Auburn, Maine; Lamin-art, Shaumburg, Ill.; Nevamar, Odenton, Md.

SOLID SURFACING
Staron, Seoul, Korea; Marlite, Dover, Ohio; Avonite, Florence, Ky.,

VINYL BASE
Johnsonite, Chagrin Falls, Ohio

WALLCOVERINGS
Lanark Wallcovering, Fairlawn, Ohio; Thybony, Chicago; MDC Wallcovering, Elk Grove Village, Ill; Metro Wallcoverings, Chicago

METAL LAMINATE
Chemetal, Chicago; Centiva, Florence, Ala.

PHOTOGRAPHY
Jennifer Nemec, Chicago

A1 Lounge
Concept Store

Vienna, Austria

INNOVATIVE STORE

Special Award

Outer space meets inner space in this theatrical three-floor, 7500-square-foot mobile-phone store. Drawn in by three computer-controlled fog machines outside, customers enter through a tunnel complete with illuminated glass floor and up a ramp to the main building. "Future Cubes" along the wall show phones of the future as holograms. Inside, fixtures that consist entirely of LCD screens can display up to five products.

CLIENT
Mobilkom Austria, Vienna, Austria

DESIGN
EOOS, Vienna, Austria – Gernot Bohmann

GENERAL CONTRACTOR
Construction Support, Vienna, Austria

OUTSIDE DESIGN CONSULTANTS
Schella Kann, Vienna, Austria (fashion design); Virgil Widrich, Vienna, Austria (sound design); YellowFish, Vienna, Austria (programming); Gunter Eder, Vienna, Austria (graphic design); Ars Electronica, Linz, Austria (animations)

FURNISHINGS
Walter Knoll, Herrenberg, Germany

LIGHTING
Zumtobel Staff Lighting, Dornbirn, Austria

MULTIMEDIA
3C! Technologies, Vienna, Austria; Creative Computing Concepts, Vienna, Austria

PHOTOGRAPHY
H.G. Esch, Hennef, Germany (lounge entrance area, fog façade, the shop, the lounge); Paul Prader, Vienna, Austria (entrance area, future ramp, the bar, the tables, the ghost mobile)

a1 lounge

og bar
conference
og news
ug shop

Apple Store Ginza

Tokyo

INNOVATIVE EXTERIOR

Special Award

The Ginza store's minimal rectilinear form and elegant materials contrast starkly with its busy surroundings. Bead-blasted stainless-steel panels mark the first three levels, while the top five floors use an open-joint, glass, rain-screen system in front of floor-to-ceiling, stainless-steel, sliding-glass doors – which also create an acoustical and weather barrier for the interior. And two custom-designed all-glass elevators add to the exterior ambiance.

CLIENT/DESIGN
Apple Computer Inc., Cupertino, Calif. – Steve Jobs, ceo; Ron Johnson, executive vp, retail development and graphic design
Apple Store Ginza, Chuo-Ku, Tokyo – Sayegusa Honkan

DESIGN/ARCHITECTURE
Bohlin Cywinski Jackson, Berkeley, Calif. – Peter Bohlin, design principal; Karl Backus, principal, project director; Anastasia Congdon, project manager

ARCHITECT/ENGINEER/GENERAL CONTRACTOR
KAJIMA Design, Tokyo

OUTSIDE DESIGN CONSULTANTS
Eight Inc., San Francisco (design associate and fixture designer); Gensler, Tokyo (design associate); Dewhurst MacFarlane & Partners Inc., New York (structural engineer); Flack & Kurtz Inc., San Francisco (MEP engineer); ISP Design, Miami (lighting design)

PHOTOGRAPHY
Roy Zipstein, New York

shoeBUZZ

The Shoppes at Blackstone Valley, Millbury, Mass.

INNOVATIVE SIGNAGE/GRAPHICS

Special Award

Signage and graphics drive the design at shoeBUZZ, a new kids' shoe store designed to make shopping fun for kids and convenient for parents. Fun fixtures feature games on side panels, creating a diversion for the target clientele. And the unique logo pervades all store signage, including the FitZone, where the "Buzz Patrol" (store personnel) checks shoe sizes.

CLIENT
Stride Rite Children's Group, Lexington, Mass. – Pam Salkovitz, president, Children's Group; Jay Nannicelli, svp, retail operations; James Harte, director, retail and construction

DESIGN
Monastero & Associates Inc., Cambridge, Mass. – Nina Monastero, principal-in-charge; Edith Twining, designer; Jonathan Merin, job captain

GENERAL CONTRACTOR
Treehouse Development, Lake Mary, Fla.

OUTSIDE DESIGN CONSULTANTS
Friskey Design, Sherborn, Mass. (graphics); Lux Lighting Design, Belmont, Mass. (lighting); Zade Co. Inc., Cambridge, Mass. (engineers)

IN-STORE GRAPHICS
ICL Imaging, Framingham, Mass.

MOBILE FABRICATOR
Unigami, Coral Springs, Fla.

INTERACTIVE TOY PANELS
Custom Surroundings, Valley City, Ohio

FIXTURES
Opto Intl. Inc., Wheeling, Ill.

STOREFRONT SIGNAGE
Colite, West Columbia, S.C.

PHOTOGRAPHY
Lucy Chen, Somerville, Mass.

Apple Mini Store

Palo Alto, Calif.

INNOVATIVE STORE LIGHTING

Special Award

Light materials and lighting maximize the diminutive space at Apple's new "mini" store. An all-glass storefront opens up the space from the entrance, while a seamless reflective floor and luminous ceiling continue the illusion. And a 20-foot-long layered, rear-illuminated graphic panel along the product wall brings the premier products to life.

CLIENT/DESIGN
Apple Computer Inc., Cupertino, Calif. – Steve Jobs, ceo; Ron Johnson, executive vp, retail development and graphic design
ARCHITECT
Eight Inc., San Francisco
ROLLOUT ARCHITECT
MBH Architects, Alameda, Calif.
PHOTOGRAPHY
Roy Zipstein, New York

Index of Design Firms

For more information on visual merchandising and store design, subscribe to:

VISUAL MERCHANDISING AND STORE DESIGN

Books on visual merchandising and store design available
from ST Media Group International:

Aesthetics of Merchandising Presentation
Budget Guide to Retail Store Planning & Design
Feng Shui for Retailers
Retail Store Planning & Design Manual
Stores and Retail Spaces
Visual Merchandising
Visual Merchandising and Store Design Workbook

To subscribe, order books or request a complete catalog
of related books and magazines, please contact:

MEDIA
GROUP
INTERNATIONAL

ST Media Group International Inc.
407 Gilbert Avenue
Cincinnati, Ohio 45202

p: 1.800.925.1110 or 513.421.2050
f: 513.421.5144 or 513.421.6110
e: books@stmediagroup.com
www.visualstore.com (*VM+SD* magazine) and www.stmediagroup.com